NEIGHBORHOOD STORIES ARIZONA

By Larry Brasen Sr.

ISBN 9781736854877

TABLE OF CONTENTS

WRITE IF YOU FIND WORK

Applying for a teaching job in Arizona was a lot different than getting any of my other jobs in Montana. In Montana I had simply heard about a job and called the school office, got an interview and got offered the job. I had never had the experience of being rejected by a school where I had interviewed.

When we decided to throw over our teaching jobs in Montana and move to the Greater Phoenix area we filled out a huge number of applications. The process was daunting to say the least. First of all there were so many School Districts. It seemed as though every few miles there was another school district. To find employment at any one of them one had to fill out an entrance application. These applications were long, detailed and each was different. They asked questions using educational jargon with which we were unfamiliar. In addition to the tediousness of the applications, including hand written philosophies of Education, we had no idea of the demographics for any area for which we were filling out the applications. We got information from the Department of Public Instruction in Phoenix for the entire state. We then ordered applications for every district in the greater Phoenix area. We started telling everyone we knew that we were moving to Arizona and asked if they knew anyone that taught down there.

One day in Eckroth Music in Billings a friend who was the instrument repairman there told me about a friend he knew that was teaching in Scottsdale. He gave me his name and phone number. That very evening I called him and had a quite informative chat. Towards the end of our conversation he said, “You know, We are going to be gone to Alaska on a sail boat for the entire month of June and from the way we talk to each other I think we would be happy to have you folks house sit for us while we are gone. We could help each other that way.” Another friend who taught Music at Bridger Montana said she had a friend who taught music in Scottsdale. She gave me her name and number. (Karen Beck) I called right away and had a wonderful chat with her. She was encouraging.

We quit our jobs in Roberts and Bridger and started evaluating our job applications. As soon as school went into the summer recess we got in our car and drove to Arizona. We got to Scottsdale and our son and Daughter in law's home on a Friday at the end of May. We visited and played all week end and then on Monday we called our contact who was willing sight unseen to loan us their home for the entire month of June. They were just going out the door for Alaska as they picked up the phone. Without ever meeting us they left the key for the house with their neighbor and we stayed in their home for free the entire month of June. Our schedule for that month was get up early and tackle another application. We bought two typewriters and sat in separate rooms writing the apps. When we finished we would read each others and comment on the jobs we had done. By Ten A.M. or so we would hand deliver the freshly finished paperwork to the district office. That would be the first time we would see the area in which we were seeking employment. Some were surprising.

Then we would grab a quick sandwich at a fast food spot and head for the University Library where we could gain access to a bank of computers so we could do research on E.R.I.C. to help fill out the next mysterious application.

After studying for a couple hours we would either return to our borrowed home and make supper and watch the television shows (There seemed to be an incredible number of channels compared to our choices in Bridger, MT.) or we might treat ourselves to a movie and home. We followed that same general daily routine most every day. The last thing we would do was make phone calls to job hotlines to see if any particular district should be the next lucky one to get our application. By the end of the month I had been called for at least three different interviews.

The first was with a district in the southern valley. The office looked new and neat. I actually was called by the Principal of this Elementary school. She was a professional looking lady and was pleasant in the interview process. Accompanying her was a male Sixth grade classroom teacher. They stated that my most important task would be to conduct the Holiday Concert in December. Since more people attended it than anything else, they wanted to know how I viewed the Holiday Concert Concept. I replied that in Roberts, Montana I had created a program for Christmas that I called the "Renaissance Christmas Review". I joyfully explained how we had read out of the King

James version of the Bible the "Christmas Story". I was encouraged as I saw them exchanging meaningful glances so I hurried on explaining how the media specialist and I had made an accompanying slide show of the great works of art from the Renaissance period and how all the students in the school from Kindergarten through grade Twelve had sung all the appropriate Christmas hymns most of which were created about that same era. They thanked me politely for my time and were most complimentary about my program concept. I often wondered why I never heard from her again.

I then received a call from an Elementary School in Scottsdale itself. I was excited. I was interviewed by a nice lady principal that I guessed was in her mid fifties. We seemed to hit it off quite well. It became apparent that the job entailed being a teacher at the Middle School also. So after concluding our chat she made a phone call to the principal of the Middle School to set up a meeting with him right away. After everything was set and we had said our good-byes and I got out to the parking lot I realized to my horror that my car keys were locked inside the car and so I had to go back to the school to use their phone to call Betty to bring the extra set of keys. Of course the front door was locked. Since time was at a premium I could feel a sense of panic gnawing at my being. Knowing that the nice lady was still inside, I ran around and found the window up high where I thought we had been conducting our interview. The fact that there was a hedge of very thorny desert bushes and the small window was at least seven feet off the ground should have given me a clue that this was not a normal window to an ordinary room. Undaunted, I began tapping at the window, standing on my tip toes in that unforgiving brush when the nice lady principal's face appeared with a look of apprehension. After indicating her surprise at seeing me in the bush, tapping on the restroom window, I was able to ask her if it would be all right to use her phone. She said that it would be okay and for me to meet her at the front door. I believe it was my confession about the keys that may have thrown her over the edge, making her more than just a little concerned about how I might interact with her students. The interview with the Middle School Principal was quite short and I never heard from him or the nice lady again.

Shortly after that I listened to the jobline recording for the Chandler School District and was excited to find they were looking for an Elementary/Middle School Band Director. Now this is really my cup of tea. While I was certified to teach all music in K-12 except the strings, I really felt my preparation had been directed towards Instrumental Music. So it was with great eagerness and anticipation that I called the number listed and asked for an interview with my prospective Principal. Sure enough a couple of days later there I was parking my car in front of a beautiful, new brick edifice with all the flower beds tidy, bushes trimmed, the neighborhood surrounding the school was made up of all brand new homes that I knew had cost a pretty penny. Making sure to remember my car keys I walked assuredly to the entrance. This looked more like a resort than a school. This must be going to be teacher heaven.

Inside I was ushered into the presence of my boss to be, a fashionplate lady in her mid thirties that I felt certain I had seen on the cover of some magazine while standing in line at the local grocery market. My mind, ordinarily incisive, logical, and fond of linear thought patterns, actually quit working for me. To see people like this in the movies, on television, on record jackets, in fashion shows was one thing. To actually be sitting in the presence of a star and being interviewed by her was something else. She started, "What would you say are your main strengths in the field of music education? What do you bring to this position that would make me decide in your favor?"

Well, I was really ready for this. At my previous jobs and particularly at my latest position in Roberts, my Band had received the highest rating at the District Music Festival and my two Stage/Jazz Bands had received the same. In fact my top Stage Band had gone on to receive one of the top ratings in the entire state later my last year before moving. I had played in Stage Bands and Jazz groups all my life, starting in Scobey, Montana, my home town, where as High School students we were always attempting to form a dance band and play for dances in the area. Then when in college at Eastern Montana College we had formed a little Jazz quartet, The Moon Glows, and had played all over the state as a way to make extra money. Oh yes, I was ready. I told her so! "How about Vocal Music?" she asked. Even her voice was of that incredible star quality. "You do teach chorus of course." As she smiled I swear I saw that glint of a sparkle shining forth from her teeth just like all the toothpaste ads I had ever watched.

"Oh, absolutely. You know I am certified in Elementary, and Middle School, and High School Instrumental as well as General Music and Chorus. But of course my real interest is in teaching band. It is where I feel the most comfortable. That is really where I am at home," was my reply.

I noticed a just ever so little hint of a frown tugging at the corners of her cosmetically perfect eyes and forehead. "Mr. Brasen, since you so obviously prefer teaching Instrumental Music and your experience has so prepared you for that field, I feel that I just have to ask you why you are applying for this Elementary Music Position." My mind snapped back. What? Is it too late? Can I do anything to save this interview? How could I have possibly...?

I excused myself and allowed her to show me to the door. That was the last I ever saw of her, but I did learn a great lesson that day. Make sure you know what job you're applying for before you begin your interview. Of course I had another experience to share with my family that night. After two or three more similar experiences I felt I was definitely getting the hang of this whole thing. I was dressed for the interviews the same as all the other applicants sitting in a row waiting for their chance to see the respective panel of judges. I had all the same smart up to date answers for all the same questions that everyone else had. We simply didn't have anything to set us apart from each other and with my fifty plus years, amount of experience and number of college credits, I was pricing myself out of each job even before I got to the interview. I decided to make a major change in my attack (if I ever got another chance.)

I got a call from Paradise Valley Unified School District. I was to go for a preliminary interview at the district office. If I passed this screening I would then be acceptable for interviews at any individual school in the district. The meeting took place and was relatively uneventful (a good thing). Later that afternoon I was called by Sandpiper Elementary School to interview for the Elementary Music Teacher position. Ten O'clock the next morning found me in a line of three or four young school teachers all sitting primly, brief case at the ready, neatly dressed waiting for the coveted interview. When it came my turn, I picked up my guitar, slung it over my shoulder and sauntered into the office where a panel of two teachers and the Principal awaited their next victim. After introductions around we were all seated and the questions began. “How might you integrate your teaching to fit with what is being taught in the regular classroom?” asked the fourth grade teacher sitting across from me. “Interesting you should ask that,” I replied, as I reached for my now ever present, trusty guitar. I explained that one day while teaching in Roberts I stepped into a Third/Fourth grade combined classroom during a break and was introduced to Shell Silverstein’s book Where the Sidewalk Ends. I created music for several of the poems in the book and my Elementary students enjoyed singing them often. With that, I burst into “Skinny McGuinn” accompanying myself with the guitar. Another question, another answer in song. I then launched my own inquisition about Student/Family demographics and a fair variety of other questions of the panel. After some time the principal, Mr. Canelake said, “Larry, if you don’t mind could we ask you just a few questions we are curious about?”

Upon reporting to my son, Larry Jr. that evening about how the interview had gone, he queried, “Dad, what is your plan B?”

“Gosh, I don’t have one”, I heard coming from my mouth.

“But Dad, you always have a plan B.”

“Hmmm.”

At Nine O’clock the next morning Mr. Canelake called saying that of all the applicants they really liked me best and if I wanted it the job was mine.

SAM'S TWINKLE ODYSSEY

Sam, our grandson, was born with the gift of music. From his earliest days in his crib Betty and I suggested that Larry Jr. and Janelle, our son and Daughter-in-law place a boom box under his bed and play Mozart and Louis Armstrong softly to help him develop his musical ear and also, as the prevalent theory proposed, to help in the proper development of the brain. From the time he was able to stand in his crib he was able to direct Mozart's Concerto from the Marriage of Figaro. Betty and I are both quite musical and so are Larry Jr. and Janelle. It was no surprise that little Sam was able to carry a tune vocally. It was a sheer joy to listen to him singing exactly on pitch with that sweet voice.

In Fourth Grade the students at Sam's grade school, Pueblo Elementary, in Scottsdale get to opt to begin either a band instrument or an orchestra instrument. The thing that I admire about the school is their commitment to the music program because the students also may opt for Elementary Chorus and still be in the Instrumental track. Sam had been shown the instruments of the orchestra (Strings) earlier at the school and had decided that he was going to play the violin. The Strings teacher, Mrs. Turner, had a relatively huge Beginning Orchestra, testifying to the quality of her teaching and the highly desirable interaction she has with her kids. From the time Sam got his first violin, "Tunie", I could see that this was going to be something special. The way he handled it-- the way he looked at it-- the way he thought about it-- even the way he closed the case after playing it--

If you have ever heard beginning violin players in their first attempts to make music, you know that even to be able to recognize Mary Had a Little Lamb is a minor miracle. We could not only recognize it, but it sounded good. There was Sam, playing a piece and correcting finger positions to bring this sometimes uncooperative instrument into tune.

After listening to just a few little pieces both Betty and I were convinced that Sam should have some private lessons. Mrs. Fisher, his wonderful first private teacher, introduced Sam to what as I recall was named "A Mozart Concerto". It was "Twinkle, Twinkle, Little Star" Theme and variations.

As we listened to him play it a couple weeks prior to the school's big talent show night, I was struck with the idea that it would be fun to play along with him on the piano here at home. I sat down and started to chord along by ear in the key of D Major. As he started to pick the speed up faster and faster I stayed right with him, ending very suddenly. I offered him a high five and caught the look of supreme satisfaction in his eyes. "Hey, Sam. Let's try doing this same thing in a Rock and Roll Style."

"What do you mean? How do we do that?"

I started laying down a slow, easy "Baby Elephant Walk" rhythm and blues left hand and just cording with the right all in D Major. "See? Here where I change to the G chord is where you play the part Little and then I go back to D when you play Star. Let's try it! One,two ready play!" I'm fairly sure "Twinkle" never sounded like that. What fun.

“You know what? We could start out with the simple, slow part, surprise everyone with the Rock and Roll, then hit ‘em with that fabulous double time part with an accelerando getting so fast it seems like nobody could ever play that fast and end with going back to the beginning, nice and easy.” I don’t know how much of that arrangement was my idea and how much was Sam’s but it was the most fun I’ve ever had making music. Until I played with my own grandchild I had no idea how it felt.

Janelle had put together a very nice piano teaching studio in their home. At this point she suggested that we do our “arrangement” together at her student’s recital coming up the next weekend. We decided to do it and after practicing it several more times we were sure we could remember the order in which the different parts came and the cues we used to get to each different section.

The big night of the recital came and I must confess I was as nervous as I can remember being about any performance. This was major. This was the Big Time. The recital was being held in the Church Sanctuary. People were getting there with their kids. Some were already seated and chatting with each other. It was about half an hour to go when Sam and I found each other. We went over the piece a couple times making sure we knew what we were going to do and it was time to go to the performance area and settle down.

Each of the students that played went through several Major Scales and a I-V-I in that key before playing their chosen pieces. As our turn approached I could feel that old familiar excitement beginning to churn. Years and years had taught me how to master that adrenaline flow, putting it to use in performance and as uncomfortable as it is in your blood, I don't believe I would want to try living without it. I glanced at Sam. He was cool as a cucumber. Did this kid have ice water in his veins? Then we made eye contact and I caught a hint of his nervous smile. Sure enough, there was some of my blood in there too.

It was a great experience, playing there together in front of that nice little crowd. We did it all correctly and were well received. After the show, Janelle suggested we might repeat the performance at Sam's private teacher's recital the next Sunday afternoon. I jumped at the chance and Wednesday found Sam and me at his private violin lesson performing for his teacher. She was excited to have something a little different for her recital and was totally accepting of the "ear arrangement" we had put together.

Mrs. Fisher, Sam's private Violin teacher, was primarily a Cellist instructor. She agreed to take Sam as a student on a limited basis. Since he was a Beginner, she would take him for his first year or two giving us an opportunity to find a suitable instructor to take over once she felt Sam needed someone for more advanced studies. Since the bulk of her students played cello, she allowed us to perform early in the program. When our time came, Sam and I trouped up on the stage, set up, and played. Our performance was once again well received and we enjoyed our brief moment in the sun.

Later, I believe it was Janelle who quietly suggested we take our show to Sam's school, Pueblo Elementary, for the big Talent Show. That is one of the biggest and best attended programs at the school. People who don't even have kids in the show attend just to watch the various talented acts. The talent show wasn't terribly long, but some of the acts made you feel as though it would last forever. Most of the kids did a wonderful job and the variety of the entertainment kept one wondering what would be next.

Sam wore his black shirt and pants. He is in my opinion an extremely attractive young man. When the spot light hit his golden hair contrasted by his formal black wear it was a sight to behold. He placed his violin, “Tunie”, under his chin and held it there with no hands. I always marvel at that. He nodded to me and we began what we thought would be our final performance of what I call Sam’s Twinkle Odyssey. We carried it off without a hitch and when we were done playing our piece for the last time the audience, which was filled with many grandparents and knew our relationship, exploded in applause.

Man! There is nothing like music. There is nothing like **making** music. There is nothing like making music with grandchildren. There is nothing like applause. I love it in every form, don’t you? When you put these all together it makes for quite a nice day.

Sam and I thought our journey with Mozart was done. Little did we know…

(To be continued)

Rick Black's Party

At first glance Rick Black might put you in mind of a possible alumnus from the Hell's Angels. He rides a motorcycle, has long white hair and a long white beard. You might say he could stand to lose a couple pounds but then couldn't most of us. It is not uncommon to see him in what appears to be black leather cycling clothes including the polished black boots. What that first glance would not be telling you is that he has a wonderfully gentle spirit or that he is a talented musician with a good voice, great ear and a feel for rhythm that only an accomplished drummer has. Also, being a Christian, he is so committed to his church praise band and music program that I am sure he personally has paid for a major portion of the electronic equipment the church has. After getting to know Rick it is impossible not to like him. Rick is constantly talking about putting together a "Blues Band". When he talks about it, it not only seems possible but highly desirable. So it was no surprise when he started talking about having a Jam Session over at his place and inviting several musician friends to have some ribs and music. He invited our Praise Band

Director Carol, the other two vocalists Dave and my wife Betty, Larry Jr., the guitar man/vocalist, Janelle our pianist/vocalist, me on Bass and trumpet.

"Can we bring the kids?" asked Janelle.

"You bet," was the reply.

It was a warm spring Sunday afternoon in Scottsdale Arizona. (Warm in Scottsdale can easily be in the 90 degree range.) Betty and I pulled the van up at the kid's home and everyone started loading up. I noticed that Sam had not brought his violin. Knowing that you can never take advantage of an opportunity to play if you don't have your ax, I said, "Hey Sam, why don't you bring Tunie with you? You never know when you might get a chance to play."

"Okay Grandpa," Sam said with a sound in his voice that indicated he might just be as happy if the chance to play did not arise.

Larry and I left in his Corvette and everyone else followed a little later in the van. When we got there I have to admit I was interested in the variety of the guests Rick had invited. There were several neighbors that did not play anything. Rick later told me that the best way to keep them from complaining about the noise was to simply have them be a part of the party. Rick's drums were all set up and the Electronic keyboard was plugged in and ready to go. There were a couple of Amps for guitars already there. We set up our Amps and equipment and set about tuning and getting out of the direct sunlight that was coming at us on about a 45 degree angle from the West. There was an older lady sitting at one of the tables, talking to Rick's mother. I could see that this cigarette smoking, thin, elderly lady with the leathery skin had been quite a pretty girl at one time. Greeting Rick's mother and introducing myself to her friend I discovered she played piano and sang with her young guitar playing friend. Walking over to him I noticed his speech was slightly slurred and he wasn't terribly steady on his feet. He switched the beer bottle from his right to his left hand so we could shake.

About this time the rest of our party drove up in the van. As the van was being parked and they were getting out, the Harmonica man started playing. I asked the piano player, "What are some of the tunes you do?"

"Just about anything, I have a couple Fake Books along," was the lady's reply.

Over at the Keyboard she started the chord pattern for Just a Closer Walk With Thee.

Now I just love that tune. "What gear ya in?" I asked, grabbing my trumpet.

"B-flat Honey," she said. A real smile started to remove some of the years that had built up on her forehead and around her eyes.

As I started to slide into that wonderfully simple old melody, I could hear the drums picking it up with a pair of brushes on the snare, accenting with the ride cymbal and the pulse of the bass drum. Now Larry Jr. is there filling with some really nice guitar blues type fill licks. The other guitar man is laying down this simple fine chord progression. Nothing fancy. Just good old simple music. One time through and that cigarette stained voice is picking up the words. "Just a closer walk with Thee, Precious Savior hear my plea." Grab your cup mute and lay in some of those easy Blues phrases that lead to the next chord change! "Take it." The harmonica is bending in and out, up and down. I've never played with a "Harp Man" that was this good. I'm struggling to keep up with him and then that peace comes in and fills my soul and I just let my fingers, lip, and breath do what they know how to do without me thinking about it and getting in the way. Several times through with everybody getting a shot at soloing and ending with everyone doing their own thing last time through and no one wanting to quit, the ending going on and on and on. Finally silence. People clapping and laughing and doing high fives and just quietly feeling good.

GOD!!! Try explaining how that feels to a non-musician.

“Hey Sam. Grab Tunie and let’s do our song.” I had already told the guys in the band about our arrangement and they were excited to make some more music, knowing how very delicate a person’s introduction to a new group and a new musical experience can be. There stands Sam with Tunie, blinking in midst of a haze of cigarette smoke and smelling the aftermath of consumed alcohol. Even the time hardened saloon musicians recognize the moment. The drums, the two guitars, the piano, harmonica, and me on the bass and Tunie making music. The second time through the pianist starts to sing along with Sam and he acknowledges her with a smile as he continues to play. Eyes of some are wet as we end.

"How long you been playing?"

"That was really cool. I can't remember the last time I sang that song."

"Boy, you are really gonna be good. Just keep practicing."

Most of us know that a Rite of Passage had just happened and Sam would never be the same. As we dropped the kids off at home later that night I noticed a spring in Sam's step that hadn't been there before, a tilt of the head that was just a little different.

"Goodnight Grandpa and thanks."

MAGIC AT SANDPIPER

Getting Started

It was the first day of school at Sandpiper Elementary. Teachers always have to report before the students arrive and I was busy in my room after attending the obligatory opening "Teachers Meeting". The room was a triangular shaped afterthought attached to the cafeteria stage by a movable wall with a door in it. The part of the floor nearest to the stage wall was a triangular hardwood extension of the stage floor that jutted into the room under the wall. Having a Minor in Educational Theatre, my interest was immediately piqued. Could we move the wall for a presentation thereby increasing the size of the limited stage? While continuing the investigation of the new teaching environment and preparing the room for instruction, I was greeted with a most welcome interruption.

"Hi. My name is Amanda."

"And mine is Connie, and we're going to be 6th grade members of the <u>Sandpiper Singers</u>."

"Do you need any help? We have some time and would be happy to work for you."

A teacher learns to always accept the offer of help from students. It's an opportunity to acquaint yourself with them as individuals and for them to get to know you more as a person than an authority figure. "You bet. Here, see these posters of famous dead white guys? We need to get them up on the walls of the room. What do you think? Tacks or staples?"

"Famous dead white guys? You're funny."

"Well, I work at it. What do you think?"

First Teaching Day

The first class of students was ushered into my room by their Sixth Grade Teacher, Bob Anderson. "I'll be back to pick them up. Please have them lined up and ready to go on time."

The big question of the year was posed by one of the bigger and more vocal boys in the class. "What is the big play at the end of the year going to be?", Asked Rick. Rick Mattheson was very polite and also insistent.

He was determined that there would be a big play to cap his Elementary School experience. “We are going to have a big play, aren’t we?”

Much to my immediate regret, my mouth responded before my brain could stop it. “Absolutely!” Oh, my God! Did I say that? How could I modify my reply to make it a little less decisive? Couldn’t I figure a way to leave a little wiggle room?

Before there was even time to continue, my first sixth grade class erupted in wild, enthusiastic applause. Giving them my biggest most positive smile I began at once to take credit for my statement. Seeing that it was a wonderfully popular concept, I began to build on it. “Do any of you have any ideas about what you might like to do for the big show?” Suddenly their teacher was there and it was the first time of many I was late getting the kids ready to return to their class.

After the Fifth Grade class under Dale Crisp got settled in my room and the roll was taken I immediately launched out on my now most popular subject, “The Big Finale Play at the End of the Year”. It was met with the same acceptance the Sixth Grade had given it. By the time I finished with the first grade at the end of the school day I figured I might just be the most popular guy in the school. Now after the last student left I allowed myself to begin to consider what I had done. Ooooowee! What Show could we do? How could we do it? What show did I know and like the best? Then it hit me. OKLAHOMA!

Sandpiper Singers

Sandpiper Singers is the name of the Extra-curricular Vocal Ensemble at Sandpiper Elementary School which is part of the Paradise Valley Unified School District in the metropolitan complex of Greater Phoenix, Arizona. In 1994 the school population had grown to the point where there had to be a new school added to the neighborhood. The resulting number of students remaining at Sandpiper made it one of the smaller schools in the district.

The Singers were scheduled to meet on Tuesday and Thursday Mornings at 8:00 A.M. We had our first rehearsal on the second Tuesday of the school year. We met on the stage in Kokopelli Hall (the cafeteria) which was connected to my music room. Nearly forty students attended. Having prepared some pieces of music I was sure the kids would like, I was ready with recorded accompaniment and a boombox. Linda DeWitt, a parent of two of the girls in chorus, attended the rehearsal and offered to be my helper for the year. Since I had never had a parent actually volunteer in that capacity, I didn't accept her offer at once. By the next morning I knew I would like her help and was concerned that not accepting her offer at once may have ruined my chance for an adult aide. I found her at school on Wednesday, before first period, and told her I needed her help for the year. Thursday she was in the wings, stage right, running the sound equipment.

CHOOSING THE SHOW

My favorite Broadway type show of all time is OKLAHOMA! Opening in the mid to late forties, it became the prototype for the Broadway shows to come for the next half century and beyond. It combined wonderfully singable music with the Romance of Good V.S. Evil, the romantic situations involving the battle of the sexes, the struggle to tame a new frontier, with the elements of classical and jazz dance with a great orchestral score. Also, the fact that I had performed in it as the character Judd, during Summer Theatre at Montana State University, Billings, (formerly Eastern Montana College) gave me an up close and personal acquaintanceship with the show.

I chatted with Linda about the possibility of preparing this show by the end of the year and discovered that she was also an artist capable of painting the set pieces (4x8 flats) we had inherited from the previous years. The decision was made and I announced it to my enthusiastic students. I purchased the complete piano score for OKLAHOMA! at a local music store and began the painstaking task of synthesizing the needed sections one note at a time. With the advent of computers one is able to create midi files using a piano type keyboard. It requires a great deal of time and not too much talent. It also requires a high level of motivation. We also watched the movie version of the play in some of our class time.

By the time we had held the Fall Quarter Concert in October, and the Holiday Concert in December we were ready to really tackle the big show. The steamroller called The Sandpiper Singers was gathering momentum. By the Holiday concert there were nearly sixty singers involved. We had several more adults joining as helpers. My friend, Nancy, who had two students in school also came to help with the logistics of performances.

We needed a choreographer. We needed more than a choreographer, we needed a dance instructor who would come in and create the great dances needed for so many of the scenes, including the "Dream Sequence" and teach them to the kids. Many of the students took dance from a local Dance Studio. I called the owner/instructor and made her an offer she found irresistible. She could do all that work for free. She agreed. I do believe that there is nothing as powerful and contagious as a positive dream.

As this juggernaut gained size my boss and good friend, Chris Canelake, and I had a meeting he called to help me form what is now known as the Parents of Note. This organization consisted of anyone who wished to be a part of the program. That included parents, teachers, grandparents, well-wishers, artists, writers, musicians, sound people from the community and basically anyone who felt they had something to contribute. Chris made sure that the group was tax exempt, and was autonomous. We would be able to take in donations and spend money in any way we needed while in accordance with the group charter.

As the show began to take shape help came from an unexpected source. Having always been a sincere supporter of the athletics in the school, I find that athletes and musicians have a lot in common. They both are basically a performance medium. I believe musicians draw on more and different sections of the brain than athletes, however, we ultimately both desire to perform for an audience. Greg Gillum, the Sandpiper P.E. instructor, came to me and offered to build a stage in front of the existing stage that would extend out into the audience some 12 feet. It would be the kind of stage that we could take down for most of the year and then reconstruct when needed at the end of the next year for what would become known as "SANDPIPER PRESENTS". Greg also took over the position of Chief Carpenter/Set builder. His highly imaginative woodworking really made the set bring the play to life. His

Railroad Crossing sign for Clairmore, Oklahoma still graces the wall of Kokopelli Hall.

MAGIC IN THE WALL

It was about this time of the year when the first assault on the movable wall reared it's ugly face. The district in it's wisdom had been going around replacing the movable wall with a permanent one. Most of the music instructors actually preferred the static wall. It provided less sound transfer from the cafeteria and few used the wall as the stage enhancing concept it was originally intended to be. When Chris told me about this I begged and pleaded for him not to allow it to happen. That would reduce drastically the flexibility of the performance area. It would take the Magic out of Kokopelli Hall's stage. In my mind that wall represented all the difference between our presentation to come and all the preceding programs given at our school or any others. Chris told me that the district was changing the wall in all the Elementary Schools that had been built on that floor plan and that we were on the district schedule to be done that summer. Once again I asked him to do whatever he could to see to it that the wall would remain. He promised he would do whatever he could.

TRYOUT RESULTS

Tryouts for specific roles were announced. Signup lists were posted and we had a landslide of kids signing up for tryouts. We had several judges in attendance at the auditions. When we finally finished I realized that we had way too many performers for the number of staring roles. After all the buildup and hype, we were going to have to turn down many deserving young actors because there just is not that many roles in the show.

Using a method of presentation I learned from Shelly Turk back in Montana I had introduced the vignette concept to my production crew. "Instead of producing the entire show we'll simply stage each of the major songs of our choosing as individual scenes. We'll costume the performers and create sets. Each piece will be a stand alone performance that can be used in or out of context."

"The problem is we don't have enough roles for the number of singers that tried out." I believe it was Linda that startled me with the concept of multiple casting. Her idea was to take advantage of the fact that each "stand alone" presentation could be treated as a skit. "We can have a different Curly for every scene he is in. We'll dress him the same and we can have different people in the role."

After much discussion and deliberation each role was cast and cassette accompaniment tapes were burned and labeled for each song/role. The kids picked up the tapes and accompanying libretto and went home practicing their parts. Now we had to figure out how to get the kids practicing together, scene by scene. Just when this began to appear as though it was an impossible task, Linda in-vented a practice schedule that took advan-tage of the lunch schedule and after school times to practice each scene individually. If it hadn't been for her grasp of details, this show might not ever have flown.

THE KOKOPELLI/CLAIRMORE TRANSFORMATION

By the time we needed to begin to deal with the logistics of selling tickets and how many could be allowed into each performance we realized that with somewhere in the neighborhood of 125 students cast that our 250 performance area would not hold the projected audience. This was when my good friend Missie who was team teaching fourth grade stepped in and created an attendance schedule. Each family would be eligible to acquire a limited number of tickets at each show and we would need to have a minimum of 3 shows. After much discussion we decided we would hold a “Dinner Theatre” on Friday night selling a limited number of tickets. Then we would have a show on Saturday night and a final one on Sunday afternoon. Since one of our participating student's parents operated a “Wendy’s” franchise fast food place we asked them if we could get a break on a typical OKLAHOMA! type meal. They cooperated and when the parents finished Kokopelli Hall had been transformed into Clairmore. Bails of hay around the room--miniature bales on the tables--leather reins, old collars, ropes, spurs, horse shoes, wagon wheels, saw horses, saddles, and every imaginable old Western artifact adorned the hall.

SOLD OUT

It was decided to charge $5 per person at the regular shows and add a certain amount to that for the "Dinner Theatre" to cover the cost of the meal to be served. We started selling advance tickets for each performance making sure everyone knew that the price of admission was a donation to the "Parents of Note" and if for any reason someone objected to paying anything they could be given tickets for as many people as possible as though they had paid for tickets. Missie was busy creating attendance charts, collecting money, counting each days attendance making sure when we sold out.

FINAL PREPARATIONS

Roz Sircle, the mother of one of the star ballet dancers, Janette, gathered a small group of talented sewing mothers and began to create the costumes for this huge cast. The total cast had grown to over one hundred kids. Many of the characters were responsible for their own costumes but many had to be created from scratch.

A tech crew consisting of 4th, 5th, and 6th graders was created to handle all the light and sound cues. Linda was in charge of them. She was on a learning curve that sometimes kept her just one step ahead of the kids.

As the performance approached Nancy became the stage manager. Mothers and fathers were shepherding kids from the front to the back to the performance area down in front on either side of the stage. We decided to place a chorus backup group on both sides of the stage down on the audience level on the sides of the extended stage. They could be there to add depth to the performances on stage and to give emphasis to sections that needed it. That way we kept as many students involved as much as we could.

The presentation

For the opening of the “Dream Sequence” we filled the stage with fog from a dry ice fog machine we were able to borrow from the district. This really created a magic ambiance in front of the nearly surrealistic set painted by Linda. We filled the stage as full of the fog as we could and then just before the curtains opened, we placed the kids on stage. As the curtains opened the fog rolled out onto the extension and then fell right down off the stage onto the floor of Kokopelli Hall. The audience recognizing the magic of the moment applauded even before the intricate dance created by our choreographer began.

Each vignette moved toward the wonderful end with all the assembled cast on stage singing the title song, OKLAHOMA!. We played to sold out crowds for each of our performances and we even sold standing room only tickets. The evaporative coolers weren't able to handle the heat from all the bodies and the stage lights. Even in the heat, the audience stayed and was very receptive. The *Parents of Note* netted enough so that I had sufficient money to purchase needed equipment and music and we continued to produce *Sandpiper Presents* for the 6 years I taught at Sandpiper.

POSTLUDE

After leaving to move to a Middle School where I would be able to work with kids who were a little older, I returned one afternoon to Sandpiper to look for some bit of stagecraft left behind. To my dismay, the district carpenter, Frank, was in the middle of replacing the movable wall.

"Frank, you're taking all the magic out of Kokopelli hall."

"Larry, all the magic left when you did", was his reply.

WOW!

Life In The Balance

The first quarter was drawing to a close for the schools in which Betty and I were teaching. Betty was busy testing, evaluating and getting ready to fill in seemingly endless pages of dots the school used for reporting the grades. I was preoccupied with the first concert of the year which was to take place that evening. The “Sandpiper Singers” were primed and ready to go and I was as nervous as I usually get prior to a performance.

We were following our usual weekday morning routine. Betty had showered and was getting ready to go to work at Stapley Junior High over in Mesa, Arizona. Mary, my mother-in-law who lived with us, was busy preparing breakfast. As I stepped from the shower and was shaving at the mirror I noticed our house cat, Carmel Corn, messing around at my feet. Bending down, I shooed him out of the bath area into the bedroom. Being somewhat myopic, I was bending forward attempting to see my face through the steam covered mirror when I felt a slight stinging sensation on my bare toe. “Ouch. What the heck was that?" It felt as though I'd been stuck with a needle.

Stepping back I lifted my foot to the level of the sink. There was nothing identifiaby wrong with the toe so I simply put my foot back down and continued shaving. Looking down, I noticed that my toes actually disappeared under the edge where the cabinet doors opened under the sink. The face in the mirror was now exhibiting a frown of curiosity. Looking more closely, raising one eyebrow slightly higher than the other, my mind said, "Hmmm. Maybe we should take a look under that lip and see if we have something down there that just doesn't belong." What could it be? Perhaps someone had dropped a needle or a tack down there that simply needed to be picked up and discarded. Maybe my toe had discovered an overlooked nail from the original construction some 25 years previous.

Throwing caution to the wind I bent down and gave it my best nearsighted gaze. I got my face right down close to the area. Squinting my eyes and finally adjusting my sight by donning my bifocals, I could see nothing that could cause what I had felt on my toe.

"Ah, of course. What I need to do is run my hand across the floor and the wooden under-lip. If there was anything there that would cause that little pin prick sensation surely my fingers would find it." Slowly I moved my hand under the overhang-probing, examining, searching-again, nothing.

Glancing in the mirror at the face which was now just mildly perplexed and obviously beginning to feel the pressures of the work day I turned to the task of finishing the morning preparation and to sit down for breakfast with Betty and Mary, before leaving for my school, Sandpiper Elementary in Scottsdale, Arizona, and early morning practice with "The Sandpiper Singers".

"Say, what is that cat doing at the bathroom door?"

"I don't know. Maybe he just needs to be fed."

While putting on my right sock I definitely felt the little pang of a rose thorn in my stocking puncturing my second toe. Rip the sock off the foot. Examine it fiber by fiber. Nothing! Oh, I know. It really is something stuck in the toe. That's it! "Hey, Hon. Where is the magnifying glass? Have you seen it?"

"Why? What's up? We need to be eating you know. It's getting late."

"I know, but where is it? Do you know? Oh, never mind, I've got it."

Nothing! Wait. Is that a little red dot the size of a pinhead on the top of my second toe? Whatever...

Shirt on. Pants on. Tie draped around my neck. Socks on (ignore the rose thorn in the right sock). Let's eat and then we just have to be off.

"Say, Betty, would you take a look at the second toe on my right foot? It's starting to feel sort of a little burning sensation like there's something in it."

"Sure, let me see. Nothing here that I can see."

"Would you mind looking with that magnifying glass? I really feel something kind of tingling."

"Oh, okay." Pause. Examine. "Nope, I don't see anything at all."

"Well, all right."

"Hey, you know what? I'm starting to feel a stinging sensation on the top of my foot.

"Do you think I could have been bitten by something? I mean, this is not pleasant."

"What could it be?"

"God, I don't know. Maybe a spider. Maybe a bug of some kind. It could have been a Black Widow. I've heard they have them down here."

"Oh, Hon, I'm sure it wasn't a Black Widow."

"Good God! It's starting to move up my leg. I can't feel my foot any more and the burning is moving up my shin bone. It's like when you hit your crazy bone only lots worse."

"What do you think we should do?"

"You call Chris at Sandpiper and tell him I'm gonna be late. Have Linda play the tapes for practice and I'm going to find an Emergency Clinic. This is getting worse and worse. I can't even feel the bottom of my leg or my foot and the burning is going up into my thigh."

Once in my car I knew I had only minutes to save myself. "I suppose it's too late now to take out that life insurance I was always thinking about taking out later." The big Lincoln Continental roared to life. Tons of metal moving rapidly became a lethal weapon in the hands of a panic stricken wild man. Unlike my mind which was doing a wonderful imitation of the confused cowboy who got on his horse and rode off in seventeen directions at once, my car was methodically, though somewhat rapidly, retracing it's steps to Sandpiper Elementary School. It had been there so many times that it just seemed to automatically repeat the motions.

Then I got it! I had passed an Emergency Clinic on the way to school many times. If I just gave Old Dobbin the reins, and kept my eyes peeled, I could arrive at the lifesaving station in time yet.

I could no longer feel anything in my leg. I slapped it sharply and was repaid with a searing pain. I am burning up. Bitten by some horrible creature. Dying in my car. No help available. Then I saw it. Oh, Lord. In huge red letters it spelled out the saving message. EMERGENCY CLINIC. I was saved. At about 45 miles an hour in the parking lot I scraped 3 years of rubber off the tires as I jammed it in park, opened the door, and tumbled out running, no stumbling for the front door of the clinic. I was saved!!!

Inside there was a strange sense of order and calm. Seeing no one in the waiting room and no one behind the welcome sign, I lurched toward the front desk. "Hello. Hello there. Is anyone here?" Ring the bell for service. Chang, Ching, Pling. **That** is a lifesaving bell? My God! I found the place and nobody's here.

With the burning sensation creeping up my right side now, I heard my savior intone nasally, "May I help you?"

"I've been bitten by something. I can't feel my leg. The burning is going up my side now. I don't know what it is but I have to admit, I'm scared."

"You say <u>you've</u> been bitten? I'm afraid there is really nothing we can do here."

"What in the world do you mean? I don't know how much longer I can last. You have to do something. Help me!"

"Gee, I wish I could but this is a Pet Emergency Clinic. Didn't you notice the sign? We can't treat humans. We are strictly veterinarian here."

"Vegetarian. What are you saying?"

"No, Vet! Vet! Veterinarians!"

"Oh. Where should I go?"

"Well, we aren't allowed to make those kind of recommendations here. It might lead to a law suit or something."

"Listen, I need help." Menacingly, "I've been bitten and if you don't tell me where to go, you may be responsible for the death of a very nice person. Try **that** for a law suit. Now, where would you go if it happened to you?"

"I would get in my car and go East on Shea over to about 90th Street and turn into the Emergency Room there."

"Thank you very much."

Jumping in my car I realized I had left it running. Throw it into gear... Step on it... More rubber gone... East on Shea... Not a red Light!!! My God!!! No one coming... Run it!!! There is the sign for the Emergency Room...

As I begin to get out of the car I notice a sign stating, "All unattended vehicles will be towed at owners expense."

Panic...

There's a parking place right behind me.

Reverse... Step on it... A resounding THONNNGGG as the car comes to a sudden, complete and final stop. I glance up at the vibrating parking lot lamp post and lamp as I make my way to the Clinic front door. Maybe no one noticed the sound and the lamp swaying back and forth. Get inside quick and get help.

At the front desk I was admitted by a very nice individual who was incidentally the parent of one of my students. They got me calmed down and assured me that since I wasn't already dead that there was a good chance that I might recover fully. They put me under observation for an unknown venomous bite and had me relax on a bed in the emergency area. I was only there a short time when I was visited by a nurse who turned out to be the grandmother of a child my daughter-in-law Janelle was baby sitting. Considering there are several million people in the "Valley of the Sun", it is always amazing to me to meet someone you kind of know.

By around One o'clock P.M. it became obvious that whatever caused my discomfort was not going to kill me so since the symptoms had regressed enough the hospital released me to bed rest. Being of sound mind, I of course descended on Sandpiper Elementary for the remainder of the afternoon, reassuring all concerned that I would live and be there that evening for the concert.

Kokopelli Hall, the cafeteria/concert hall, was packed with expectant kids, parents, teachers, grandparents, and well wishers. With ten minutes left before the start time "The Sandpiper Singers" left the Physical Education Room where they had assembled and went row by row onto the stage. They performed sans director. I had been told not to do anything that would create increased blood flow so I directed "in abstentia" from the back of the auditorium. Linda, looking wonderfully fresh, worked the boombox from the wings stage right. Everything went just as it should and at the end of the concert the kids gave me a certificate commemorating the "Absent Director Concert" and Betty and I gave Linda a nice bouquet of flowers for all the work she had done including holding a rehearsal by herself.

Finally, the evening with the kids and parents was over and it was time to return home where, in the kitchen, Carmel Corn brought Betty and me a present. He proudly displayed a live scorpion he had caught in the bathroom. Not very big, but lethal enough to cause a real panic. One thing about it, if Carmel Corn ever required emergency treatment, I sure knew exactly where to take him, providing I didn't panic.

OUR LITTLE BASEBALL BALLERINA

Holly looks just a little surprised. Not displeased really, not terribly excited, just a little surprised and full of questions. "Is this what this is all going to be about?" her face asks. "And just how does this work and who in the world are you?" She is all red and wrinkly, has no hair and Sam laughs. His smile is unusually broad, his eyes flash as he views his brand new sister, and with his arms wrapped around his father's neck, at two years of age he is visibly vibrating all over.

At about one and a half years of age Holly and I are developing a wonderful relationship. I go over to visit and she drops everything she is doing to run to me saying, "Pom Pa. Pom Pa." I grab her up in my arms and squeeze and dance around in circles. Later in our time together she insists that I do "Ride the Horsey". She climbs up on my knee and it is a wild, wild ride with her screaming and laughing and as soon as I quit it is, “One more time, Pom Pa. One more time.” Then comes what has to be my favorite part of all. It is called Peek-a-boo. Holly sits in one chair and I sit in the chair beside her. I cover my eyes with my hands and removing them very quickly I say, “Peek-a-boo.” During this time my eyes get as wide open as possible. I marvel at the simple innocence as she repeats exactly as I have done. Holly’s reaction is simple imitation. My guess is that this is just another way kids learn how to act and maybe life is learning one simple lesson at a time. She is the cutest child to ever grace my life.

Holly is one of the most positive, friendly, loving, adventurous, talented young girls I have ever known. When you put that together with the looks of an angel you have a combination that can’t be beat. This all comes from a completely unbiased individual, her grandfather. She is also one of the most determined people in the world. Once she decides she is going to do something, she puts herself into it full force.

The Last Ball Game of the Season

Betty and I are already perspiring from the relatively short walk from the car to the ball diamond. It is early June in Scotts-dale and I can feel the heat of the sun pouring it's goodness on the onlookers as well as the participants. I put on my dark glasses and lost 10 degrees. We carry our own chairs from the car and that contributes to our reaction to the temperature. I check to make sure my NASA cap is on straight. I always hope someone will ask me if I was an astronaut. I have my story ready just in case but for some reason no one ever does.

After setting up the chairs and getting my super Hot Dog with all the trimmings, I hear the old familiar, "Play Ball." We are just in time to see our granddaughter Holly, now nine years old, trot proudly out to first base. Holly has always had the gift of graceful athleticism. Her somewhat spare frame allows her to accomplish some feats that her chub-bier classmates are unable to perform. Her intensity is exhibited by her stance. She leans forward in anticipation, tapping her fist in her glove, as the first pitch loops toward the batter. The ball drops right through the strike zone and the batter takes a cut at it. The ball goes foul down the third base line and the batter returns from first base, picking up his bat on his way. I yell out instructions to Holly between bites of Polish Sausage, gulps of Diet Pepsi, and moving my chair a little further into the shade, "You've got them on the run now girl. Don't get too far away from the base."

The next pitch is on its way. The air is shattered with the strength of the blow. The grounder skips right past the shortstop who watches in surprise as it bounces along. Suddenly, as if he just realizes what is happening and what his response should be, he turns and gives chase. The left fielder, who is playing not too far behind the shortstop comes charging the ball. Putting his hand in front of his face and aiming his glove at the ball through the webbing he pounces. The ball, as if it has a life of its own, continues unimpeded along its course. By this time the third baseman and the center fielder both start to get in on the action. The ball comes to a rest. The center fielder runs to it picking it up holding his prize aloft proudly. The batter, now a base runner, showing no intention of holding up, is just rounding second base.

"Throw the ball, Throw the ball," yells the coach.

“Throw the ball,” yell the players.

“Throw the ball,” Yell the parents.

“Throw the ball,” I yell, spilling my Pepsi as I stand.

He throws the ball to **first** base.

Holly actually catches the ball. She makes a wonderful throw to home as the runner is just approaching. The catcher who has become interested in her shoelaces doesn’t notice the ball or the runner.

“Get the ball, Tag him out!”

She glances up in time to see the runner’s foot touching home as he runs by to the cheers of his team mates and the fans in the stands. The first of many bona fide in-the-park home runs.

Baseball, as played by this younger set, lacks the motor skills which they are just beginning to learn through this wonderful experience. It resembles baseball but once the ball is put into play by hitting it, all resemblance to the game ends. It appears as though the children are horribly handicapped physically and mentally. Since they are just learning the nuances of the game and the physical reactions required to handle the ball, it would be fair to say that there are quite a few mistakes made. The thing that's important is that the kids are learning teamwork, fair play, and enjoying physical activity while developing needed skills. Some had been couch potatoes in their previous lives. The parents are understanding and supportive. The coaches are the best, making sure all the players get a chance and are encouraged all along the way. Each game has a time limit so the next teams can take the field. Also, after they go through the lineup once in the inning they call the other team up to bat.

The next batter hits the ball to the pitcher who knocks it down and picking it up throws to Holly on first base. Holly, jumping high in the air to catch the ball has her foot still in the air when the runner gets there. He is called safe. I personally, having the advantage of seeing the play from a slightly different angle and the added plus of sitting in the shade, am sure there is a mistake made on the call and the runner is out. That from the unbiased section! Holly has really improved her catching skills. That is a tough catch and most of the kids would have allowed extra bases by missing the ball.

The play for the next batter is out at first. Holly catches the ball when it is thrown to her and her foot is on the bag.

Soon the side is retired and Holly's team is up. Their batting skills, while improving dramatically during the season, just don't stand up very well this inning. It is basically three up and three down.

It is during the next inning that Holly makes the most incredible play of the game. She is playing a little off the first base when a line drive is hit between first and second. She reacts like a little pro. She takes two steps to her right and dives for the ball, stopping it with her bare right hand. Grabbing the ball quickly she runs over to the base and tags the runner out before he gets to first. I figure she doesn't want to take any more chances with having the ump call the runner safe when she simply steps on the bag.

During the remainder of the game Holly hits 2 for 3. Hitting has been her weak spot but her dad had helped her out with batting practice and the coach had helped all the kids with special batting practices held on Sunday afternoons. She also gets to put two more people out at first during the duration of the game.

At the end of the game, the coach awards the coveted “Game Ball”. When the time comes for this I make sure I am hanging around the area with the team and coaches. I can’t wait to see if Holly will get the award. When he says, “Well, it’s time to award the last game ball of the season.” A lot of the kids on the team start chanting, “Hol-ly, Hol-ly, Hol-ly.”

“Now, now,” The coach says. “First of all, Baily had one of her best days today. She batted 3 for 3 and caught a fly ball.” All the kids quiet down and nod their heads except for one little overactive boy who is still saying, “Hol-ly...” “Then,” the coach continues, “Melinda got her first hit of the year. Let’s hear it for Melinda.” That is followed with a chorus of cheers. “But for the overall out-standing player of the day I have to choose Holly. She did her personal best today at the plate hitting 2 out of 3. She put 4 out at first. And then if that wasn’t enough she stopped a line drive barehanded and put the man out at first. The “Game Ball” today goes to Holly!”

The Dance Recital

The hum of talking and the excited chatter of young performers spills out of the family room of the church where the dance recital is being held. Betty and I are just barely on time.

"Say Hon, did you remember the camera?"

"You mean you didn't?"

"We're not that far away, let's just turn around and pick it up."

Why is it that a two minute trip back and a one minute run into the house and back takes at least ten minutes?

"Do you see Janelle or the kids anywhere?"

"Well, I went ahead and got this bouquet for Holly and she really needs it before the performance, not after."

"Let me see what I can do to locate her and why don't you find chairs for us? Did Larry say he would be here early to save chairs?"

"No. He had to work late."

"Give me the camera and the flowers and you go get us seats. Save for Sam and Larry and Janelle."

"There's Janelle. She's up there at the piano. She told me she is going to play her original composition for Miss KatieBug's dance tonight."

Going through the door to the backstage area I am greeted with the nervous voices only a performer would recognize as the adrenaline laced little people shortly before "Going On". A shriek! "Grandpa." Holly is running to me as she always does, arms outstretched, huge smile on her face, and jumping up knowing I will catch her in my arms and hug her to pieces.

On the floor the bouquet is scattered and disorganized. My camera is hanging precariously from my neck. The stage makeup on Holly's face takes me by surprise. I first learned the art of stage makeup at Scobey Elementary School where I took part in my first "play" as Chief Rain-in-the-face. I believe it was in Third Grade that I proudly danced around the make believe camp fire saying, "Hie-ya-ya-ya, hie-ya-ya-ya," secretly hoping the wonderful head dress my mother had made didn't fall off. I hoped no one in the audience would notice that I had girl's stuff on my face. Stage moms had helped apply it. I was sure that from then on I would take care of these things myself. Still, to see my pristine Granddaughter made up like that is a kind of a shock to me. In addition to the makeup she has a beautiful flower face-painted on her cheek. Her delicate butterfly wings do not get in the way.

"Holly, stand over there with your flowers and let me get your picture." Holly steps to the side and gives me that perfect dental-brace smile. I have finally decided that since the parents are paying big bucks for the braces let's get them in the picture.

"How are you? Do you need anything? Are you ready tonight?"

"Thanks Grandpa. No, I'm O.K."

Pictures taken. Seats reserved. In place. Lights down. Betty and I are seated with Sam and Larry Jr., with a chair for Janelle when she could get there, the Dance Recital begins.

The youngest of Miss Katiebug's students have only been walking for a short time, let alone dancing. One young dancer's diaper is hanging out of her Tutu. As they twirl precariously on the downstage area I notice several parent volunteers following the whirling dancers in front of the stage. I refer to these moms as "Catchers". One little girl stops dancing and just stands there waving at someone in the audience. It's certainly a good thing they are so cute.

As the age of the participants and the years of experience with Miss Katiebug increases the dancers become more graceful and fluid on the stage. The years have a telling affect. Holly's turn is finally next. She is dancing with 3 other young friends about her age. All four of them are dressed as butterflies and as they float so effortlessly around the stage I suddenly realize that I am at a loss to understand this event in my young granddaughter's life. It is difficult to understand how she could have been the hero of the baseball game just the night before, with all the outs on first, the hits, the fabulous bare-handed stop, receiving the game ball and here tonight be floating inches above the stage to Tchaikovsky's Dance of the Sugar Plum Fairies. What kind of metamorphosis has taken place? I realize that the concept of metamorphosis is additionally appropriate because she is dressed as a butterfly. I am struck with awe at this transformation.

Then it hits me! The same intensity, the same discipline, the same physical effort, the same dedication and exertion go into both activities. Our little girl has not gone through some mystical transformation in one day. She is no longer a little baby girl playing Peek-a-boo with her grandpa. Already, at nine, she is a complex young lady willing to give of herself whatever is required in order to fulfill her dreams. Part of me longs for the little peek-a-booer, but I am truly overwhelmed with this much greater sense of being allowed to participate in her unfolding story.

TYLER O.

SANDPIPER ICE CREAM SOCIAL

Ice cream! What kid or adult doesn't go for ice cream? With that in mind Chris Canelake, our Elementary School Principal, through the tender mercies of the P.T.O., provided gallons of vanilla for the evening. This was a gathering of teachers, kids, and their parents in Kokopelli Hall, the cafeteria, just prior to the first day of school. The intention was for all the interested parties to get acquainted with each other. It was my second year as music teacher at Sandpiper Elementary School in Scottsdale, Arizona.

I partook of my share of the cold, wonderful stuff, and schmoozed with the parents of my chorus kids, retiring soon thereafter to the relative quiet of my music room. The music room door, located just off Kokopelli Hall, could be left open as an invitation to any who wanted to chat privately. This allowed me to overhear the activity in the main area, alerting me to any situation that might require my attention. Tomorrow was the first actual day of school and I was putting the finishing touches on my room. I was suddenly aware of a student quietly watching from the doorway. “Hi, Tyler. What cha up to?”

“Oh, Mr. B. I just thought I'd stop by and say hi,” replied Tyler.

Tyler was a quiet, thoughtful fourth grade girl. Intelligence flowed from her eyes in an unassuming way that caught anyone in their gaze and held them there, as though waiting for some possible revelation. She walked into the room toward the CD player. “Would it be okay if I sing a little while you work?”

I realized she had never sung an actual solo for me as a third grader so I said, “Sure. What do you have in mind?”

“I noticed in the music book last year, that One Moment In Time is in there. Could I sing that for you?” she asked.

“You bet. Did you notice which level it was in?”

Since I encouraged the students to browse in the entire music library I wasn't surprised when she answered, “Yes, I believe it was in the Sixth Grade book.”

“Let me see. Ya. Here it is. It's available with voices on the background or with accompaniment only. Which would you like?”

“Oh, I can sing it without any voices on the disc.”

The instrumental strains of Whitney Houston’s mega-hit began to replace the hubbub of the cafeteria. It was at that moment that I was totally taken aback by the purity of the voice that came drifting on top of the orchestral track. Sitting down on a chair intended for someone less well endowed in the posterior, I allowed myself to be taken to the heights this gentle pop tune reaches by this young performer.

“Tyler, where did you learn to sing like that?”

“I don’t know, Mr. Brasen. Did you like it? Was it okay?”

“Why didn’t I know you could sing like that? I mean you’ve been in my class for a full year. How could it be I hadn’t heard you sing?”

“I guess I just didn’t ever volunteer to sing for you before.”

“Well, Okay. You are going to be in Sandpiper Singers, aren’t you?”

"Yes. I've really been looking forward to it. I just love to sing."

A DEFINING MOMENT

The year progressed. The Sandpiper Singers had a concert presentation at the end of every quarter. To end the Fall Concert, Tyler stepped forward to the microphone and performed the solo part of the song she had sung for me during the Ice Cream Social. As the ending notes of *One Moment In Time* drifted out, blessing the audience with a sublime combination of Tyler's voice, the Sandpiper Singers, and the recorded accompaniment, the assembled Moms, Dads, and extended families gave Tyler and the Chorus a rousing ovation.

APPLAUSE, APPLAUSE

The next morning before school, Tyler dropped by my room. After greeting each other with the normal pleasantries, Tyler asked, "Mr. Brasen, could I ask you a question?"

"Sure, Tyler. What's up?"

"Last night. After we were all done, you know? Well, did you notice how everyone was clapping? And when you introduced me and everyone clapped—Well, I don't know if I was supposed to or not, but I just loved it. You know? I mean the clapping. I just love it when they clap for me. What do you think? Is it okay to love it that much?"

"My dear young friend. I know exactly what you mean! And yes, it is okay to love it like that. That is one of the big reasons we perform-to get that response from the audience. Always remember this—as long as you put the needs of the audience first, you can look forward to getting that reward from them. You do it to reach out and touch those people you sing for in a way that helps them through their day. When you do that, they will love you and tell you so in every way they can."

"Thanks Mr. B." Tyler turned and walked out of the room. The stages of the valley were waiting. The stages of the world are waiting.

EPILOG—NINE YEARS LATER

Nine years later I received this note in the District mail.

Mr. Brasen,

Well I graduate high school in less than a month. I’m not going to college right away, but I was cast as a lead performer on the Disney Cruise Boat, then it’s off to L.A. to try my hand at Hollywood. I wanted to say that without you and your morning choir rehearsals at Sandpiper, I never would have realized that I could sing. You were the first person in my entire life to believe in me, and give me a solo in One Moment In Time. Thank you for bringing music and performing into my life. Not a day goes by that I'm not grateful. I know you continue to do the same for hundreds of kids every day. Thank you for the music.

Tyler

SOLO NIGHT

at

SANDPIPER ELEMENTARY

and

DESERT SHADOWS MIDDLE SCHOOL

OKLAHOMA

On my first day of teaching at Sandpiper Elementary School the dye was cast. We (the kids and I) were going to have a big show for the last of the year. I decided we would do the Broadway Show, OKLAHOMA! In vignette style. Each major song in the show would have it's own cast and setting. I input the entire piano score one note at a time. I tell the story of how the whole show came to fruition in another little tale. The part to tell here was that the incredible Par-ents of Note (mostly Moms) helped with creating a practice schedule that had students coming to practice with me at specific times before, after and during school. The main time for these prac-tices was during the lunch time in my room. (My lunch and theirs) And so was born what I discov-ered to be the most productive teaching and bonding time I ever found. Eating together and practicing in front of each other came to be a ma-jor social blending for all the participants. If it hadn't been for my parents coming up with the most complex practice schedule in the world for everyone, the luncheon solos would never have been discovered. Every student learned his/her part and the show sold out to two evening per-formances and a Sunday Matinee. It was a huge money making success for my Parents of Note which gave me a financial autonomy unheard of in any of the other Elementary School Music Departments in the district.

SOLO NIGHT

From the very beginning of my second year at Sandpiper, I carried the luncheon solo program forward. I spent the summer getting cassette recordings of individual songs from Disney and Warner Bros Cartoon Musicals. They were on twenty minute cassette tapes (Ten minutes on a Side), I put the accompaniment only on the side A and the Vocal/Instru-mental on side B. By the time school started I had about 30 songs ready to go. With copies of the solo pieces in an alphabetical tub, the students could page through the choices and bring me the piece they would like to try. I would dig the appropriate cassette out of my two 3 by 5 card drawers, make a fast copy with my copier, and give it to the student to take home. From there, if the student wanted to listen to the tape and try to sing along he/she could. If not, they could just take it home to play and practice in the privacy of their own room. It was theirs to keep courtesy of the Parents of Note. For the third quarter of the year we had over twenty soloists ready to perform for our first Solo Night. I have never seen so many kids willing and able to perform vocal solos. To me, Solo and Ensemble participation is the height of Music Performance Education. It is where the rubber meets the road. Growing up in an instrumental environment it was expected that kids would play a solo on their horn and if they blew a few notes, well after all they were just kids. But if a vocal soloist was off key or didn't feel the rhythm it seemed like their world just caved in around them. It occurred to me that I should take the instrumental approach to vocal solos. I have seen more kids blossom and grow right before my eyes through this medium than any other. Athletics is probably the only other place that affords such leadership training potential. I personally feel Music is a little more cerebral and emotionally satisfying.

My last year at the Elementary School, Solo Night was attended by SIXTY Soloists, twenty from each fourth, fifth and sixth grade. I had to schedule them in one hour sessions for each grade level all in one evening. We allowed 3 minutes for each solo from five-thirty PM to six-thirty PM and so on for each grade level. We graduated more 6th grade students who knew they could sing and were willing to try out for parts than I could count. The rest of this story is about a particular student that represents what I'm talking about.

MACY

After teaching at the Elementary level in Paradise Valley Schools for six years I decided I would like to move to Desert Shadows Junior High School where my graduates went after leaving Sandpiper. At what had become the annual Fall Meeting of the Parents Of Note, I met a remarkable lady named Kim. Part of the meeting was the election of new officers of the club. With the busy life schedules these parents had there were not too many hands being raised to volunteer for the president of the club. In fact, Kim was the only one to stand right up. Later that evening, after the meeting, Kim told me that she had seen our Sandpiper Singers on stage at an Elementary School Concert and that she had decided at that time that I was the teacher she wanted for her daughters in Junior High. Up until that time my former president, Sheri had been with me for several years. Since she no longer had a student in the group, she stepped down and made room for a new CEO.

At the end of the year we were scheduled to take over sixty kids to Disneyland to perform, attend a superb seminar and enjoy the park as a reward for a successful year. At the final concert of the year which we held at Horizon High's Concert Hall, the fact that we didn't have enough money to pay for some of the kids from homes of more modest means came to light. Kim jumped up on the stage and encouraged folks to reach into their pockets and make it so all the students could attend if they wished. She told them to get up out of their seats and go out front and write checks payable to Parents of Note. They did and every kid got to go.

Prior to the beginning of the next year Kim asked for a private chat with me. Of course my curiosity was piqued and I agreed. She told me that she had another daughter coming into our school. She said, “Larry, her name is Macy. I don’t know why, but she has told me that she will never sing a solo as long as she lives. No matter what, she refuses to even talk about it. I don’t know what you can do to get her to sing. All I know is that if you’ll just keep an eye out for her and work some of that magic of yours, maybe you can to get her to perform. I know she has a nice voice and a good ear. I just can’t understand it. I know you have a lot of kids to reach but please see if there is anything you can do.”

After a couple of weeks into the school year we had our lunch program really beginning to roll. One day I noticed that Macy came in with a friend of hers. They both brought their lunch in to eat with all the kids starting on solos. I watched as the two girls made their way to the “Lead Sheet” tub.

I could see they were discussing some of the solos. Macy's friend picked a solo and came over to where I was seated behind the sound equipment. She showed me the song and I started digging into my cassette drawers. As I was fumbling around looking for the cassette I mentioned to her that the song she had chosen could be sung as a duet. At that point Macy said, "If I take the tape does that mean I'm saying I'll sing a solo in front of people?"

"Macy, all we do here is help kids get songs they like. Because of the Parents of Note, you don't have to pay anything and you don't have to commit to anything. I just like to help kids get their music."

Macy and her friend both walked out of the room that day with the music they wanted.

They both became "regulars" at my musical luncheon. After just a few days, they did their first "duet" together. For Macy, it was the beginning of a new way of thinking of herself. Soon she was trying solos for herself. She, like so many kids in the seventh grade, had a beautiful voice. Soon she was putting the emotion into her singing. She started trying out and getting solo spots in seventh grade girl's chorus.

She tried out for the select 8th grade choir and made it in. When she graduated from the eighth grade and moved to Horizon High she was one of the stars in Katie's High School Chorus for all four years. She then moved on to the University of Arizona, in Tucson. When she graduated from that institution one of the jobs I heard of her obtaining was set design on a famous T.V. show and also working in a design company supplying costumes for Hollywood. Both jobs require a healthy self image. Did participation in Solo Night help in the formation of that?

***** ***** ***** ***** ***** *****

Sometimes I think that teaching music isn't as much about "THIS IS A QUARTER NOTE! THIS IS A STAFF!" as much as it's about creating an environment in which people can discover themselves and grow in a positive direction.

RUSSELL

Russell trudged into the room. He was bent forward, counter-balancing the twenty pound weight of the book bag. He was late for his first day of Beginning Melody Men, the Seventh Grade Boys Chorus elective. The other boys, already seated in the room, paid him little attention. They were concerned with "Who are you? Who am I? How do we all fit in here?" Without saying anything he made his way to a chair separated from the other students and some distance from me. Since it was the first day of school and the Seventh Grade students were still discovering the best navigational paths to the Music room from their previous class, I didn't mention anyone's tardiness.

As day melted into day and week into week, some patterns began to evolve. Russell was usually late to my class. He began to respond to the taunts of the other boys with a negative attitude. Even when greeted by, "Hi, Russell. How ya doin?", his face, clouded with what appeared to be anger and dislike, he would respond,"You just be quiet now or I'll report you for harassment. I know who you are and I have asked you to quit."

In meeting with his parents I asked all the questions that occur to a teacher when faced with a situation of this nature. I felt that it was beyond my personal power to help him. I suggested that they might want to consider taking him to a psychiatrist or some professional that might be able to set him on a path of acceptable behavior. Of course they said they would definitely consider the suggestion, but I knew they weren't going to do anything like that.

I talked to my Assistant Principal and good friend, Ken, about Russell. "Ya know, this kid, Russell, is very strange."

"Yah, but then don't you call all your kids "Strange"?

"Well, yes. That is true, but this kid is truly different. Do you have any suggestions that could help him fit in just a little bit better?"

A frown furrowed Ken's forehead. "You say the other boys set him off during the period with you?"

"Yes. They do," I answered.

"Maybe if you have a talk with the boys when Russell isn't there, you could get them to quit pushing him so hard."

"Ya, I'll give that some thought. That won't be the easiest talk to do. I'll work on that."

I had that talk with the boys when Russell missed school soon after that. I ended it with the concept that everyone at one time or another just wants to be left alone. That's what Russell wants right now from all of you. What could be so hard about just leaving him alone?

From that day on things began to get a little better for Russell. There were days when he blew up but for the most part, Russell and the boys started getting along better. They even sang together with animated choreography.

FAST FORWARD ONE YEAR

As Eighth graders I had a unit of Melody Men II. Sure as the world, in my first Melody Men II of the year, there sat Russell. I noticed right away that Russell seemed to behave better than he had as a Seventh Grader. It was as though he had actually learned something in the previous year that he carried forward to the present.

As the semester progressed and we were planning for the Fall concert, I had chosen a song from Disney's Aladdin for the M M II. The name of the tune was "One Jump Ahead". It's kind of an enjoyable piece featuring all kinds of mischief that Aladdin could stir up. To balance that song out I chose "A Whole New World" from the same Disney show for my Eighth Grade Girls Chorus. That song could be treated as a duet, one boy and one girl. Who tried out for the boy's part? You guessed it. If it hadn't been Russell, why would I be telling this story?

When the Eighth Grade girls tried out for the Princess role, they didn't know they would be singing a duet with someone from the Melody Men. A girl named Becka was chosen for that part. When she found out that it would be a duet with Russell, she asked for a private conference with me. "Mr. B," she stated. "I don't really want to sing this duet with Russell. Can you please find someone else to do it?"

I said, "Becka, I know you to be one of the nicest people in the school. You always come to the defense of others. You would never hurt another student's feelings. You are going to have many solo experiences in your life. This may be Russell's one chance. Do this for yourself so that in years to come you can tell about helping the boy experience his one big chance."

"Okay, Mr. B. I'll do it. We don't have to pretend to be in love or anything like that, do we?"

"No. Just use that beautiful voice of yours and enjoy the spotlight."

THE BIG NIGHT

Russell made sure his folks were in the audience but they didn't know he had the lead part in the final number. The boys sailed through their song complete with animated choreography. The boys sat down on their risers while the girls stood on theirs and performed their piece. Following that the boys and girls both stood for their final part of the concert. The two spotlights came up to reveal Becka on the left and Russell on the right. They both really killed it. The audience was aroar with applause.

After that successful showing, Russell was willing to participate in other classes. It literally changed his life. On the final day of school he came up to me after all the other kids had left the room and he said, “I love you Mr. Brasen.” Shaking his head, unable to control his tears, he gave me a big hug.

EPILOG

A note from Russell’s parents:

Mr. Brasen,

Just a note to let you know how much we enjoyed the chorus concert last night. You have done an incredible job with the kids! We especially want to thank you for all the help you have given Russell. He said he had the time of his life last night. Being able to get up in front of a crowd without being afraid will benefit him his whole life.

Thank you again and have a great rest of the year!

Russell’s Parents.

www.ingramcontent.com/pod-product-compliance
Ingram Content Group UK Ltd.
Pitfield, Milton Keynes, MK11 3LW, UK
UKHW020138250726
13967UKWH00002B/738

9 781736 854877